£500 A Line and Other Poems

I0104035

Liz Bentley

chipmunkapublishing
the mental health publisher

Liz Bentley

Published by
Chipmunkapublishing
PO Box 6872
Brentwood
Essex CM13 1ZT
United Kingdom

http://www.chipmunkapublishing.com

Copyright © Liz Bentley 2010

Chipmunkapublishing gratefully acknowledge the support of Arts Council England.

Author Biography

Liz Bentley is a writer, poet, comedienne, host, programmer, musician, mother, psychotherapist and insomniac. She was born in Essex in 1964 and moved to London at 21. She lives in Peckham with her two children and fiance.

Liz sought psychotherapy at 23. Struggling with bulimia, drugs, relationships, abuse and the diagnosis of Multiple Sclerosis, her therapy allowed her to be creative and provided a way of making sense of her difficulties.

During her analysis she trained as a counsellor. She now works as a psychotherapist in primary care in Southwark, has a private practice and is one of the quirkiest voices on the UK's spoken word scene.

Since winning Short Fuse Poetry Idol, then Poetry Idol the Rivals in 2003, Liz's writing and performance has gone from strength to strength. Armed with her Casio keyboard and ukulele she has been featured at events such as Ledbury Poetry Festival, London Literature Festival at Southbank and Alternative Village Fete, National Theatre. She has had three successful Edinburgh shows (2008 being in Edinburgh's only swimming pool venue, a solo show then hosting over 100 other writers/performers in the pool).

Liz's experiences of mental health and multiple sclerosis have taken her into disability arts, performing at events such as Bonkersfest, Mad Pride, Mad Chicks, Liberty festival (Liberty laureate 2009), Da Da festival and therapy conferences. She strives to smash the apartheid between disability and mainstream arts.

www.lizbentley.co.uk

Liz Bentley

£500 a line - Comfortably

I complained about his dick tion

But I loved his stroke

He was paralysed right down his right side

But he could do double with his left

With slurred speech he told me to fuck off about my complaint about his dick tion

We walked through Peckham Rye Park

I hate walking. He loves walking with three-pronged stick

Like Jake the Peg, diddle, diddle, diddle, de

Hung to left

It was a full moon. We fucked on the bowling green

Liz Bentley

Shopping at Sainsbury's with a small child

I put him on the Bob the Builder Ride
I inserted twenty pounds in 50 pence pieces into the slot

A Smaller Place

I've been studying aeroplanes and how airhostesses
deliver refreshments via trolleys.
On my next flight I will time their comings and goings
and at a point at which all toilets are blocked from all
seated passengers we shall be in the toilet queue and
become members of the mile high club.

The toilets are small but so am I and we have managed
in the very small ones on trains.

Is trolly dolly an abusive term for an airhostess?

As a child I wanted to become a trolly dolly but I was
deemed too short. I probably like to call trolly dollys
trolly dollys because I envied them. They had
something that I could never have had at their age.

For all I know a certain height may not be criteria for this
position now but I'm 45 now and the job doesn't appeal
to me anymore.

I was also too short to become an ambulance person.
They told me that it would be a problem carrying
stretchers. "We don't want patients sliding off," they
said.

I asked them why they couldn't employ two people of
small height and then this wouldn't be an issue. They
said "but what would happen if one went off sick?
Sickness is a huge problem in the NHS."

Liz Bentley

A small quiet place

We slept on the doctor's couch in the Marie Stopes
abortion clinic
In the morning we had a cup of tea
I hoped that the manager wouldn't wonder how comes
the kettle was warm

A small dark place

I was driven off the autoroute and into a forest
The bunk behind the driver's seat was small, narrow
and uncomfortable
But not as uncomfortable as the knife could have been

The shame of being a tsidohteM

Balance your collection on the rim of Mrs Ager's hat
When she notices take the collection
When Mrs Ager takes off her hat and balances it on a
peg and goes into the main church
Take collection for all departments of the Sunday school
Play Frisbee with Mrs Ager's hat then get pissed on
blackberry juice in the kitchen and steal the collection
for real alcohol.
When Mrs Ager returns with the other children from the
main church get into Bible Corp groups
Think about the greedy Jew who climbed up a tree and
stare at a picture of the black missionary man who is
coming to visit next week
No black men in our town, just an Indian girl at school
Mrs Ager's husband Mr Ager told my sister that when
she grows up he's going to marry her
Mr Ager died before my sister was old enough, but Mr
Ward our history teacher married Haidee Fill when she
was sixteen
Mrs Ager now has a budgerigar who enjoys her piano
playing

Separating from my eleven year relationship and the father of my two children ages 2 and 8

"I'm thinking of separating," I said
"Oh ok," he said

London Bridge is falling down

My leggings had lost their freshly washed firmness and were slipping down at Peckham Rye Station

I lifted up my dress and pulled them up

I thought I'd been discreet, but somehow my exhibitionist self had subconsciously slipped out onto the platform full of people including a stationmaster, all of whom had received a not –so- private viewing of my arse

"Oh, I'm sorry," I said, "I didn't think anyone was looking"

The station master smiled and asked whether I was comfortable now

"Yes thank you," I said

On the train to London Bridge I wondered how much of a difference there was between this, and the man I'd seen on the bus adjusting himself, reading Nuts

Sexual Health Clinic

I went up to the receptionist of the Sexual health clinic
and said "Hello"
She looked at me and smiled and said
"I'm always eating a sandwich when you come here
You must think I'm a right pig"

Valentines day

Valentines day
Valentines day
Don't ever go away,
Don't go away because I want you to stay
Not because I like you
But because I like things I don't like

My boyfriend uses his pedometer every day
I told him he should wear it in bed
He told me it rattles and is disinclined to wear it in bed

Valentines day, Valentines day, don't buy me flowers
today
You will pay more than they will cost tomorrow

All I want for Christmas is a shelf put up

Rugby

My father had jockstraps which he left hanging around
the house

Liz Bentley

I shouldn't be left on my own for long or I may self-harm

Last night I watched Katie Price and Peter Andre
Unleashed
 I laughed with them

£500 A Line and Other Poems

Aunt Margaret needs a new cardigan

I want a neutral colour
What do you mean?
Beige
If they haven't got beige, what colour do you want?
A neutral colour
What colour is a neutral colour?
You know, a neutral colour
If I go into a shop and they don't have beige, should I
get black or white or blue?
Grey
If they haven't got beige I'll get grey
I don't want the buttons going all the way up to the neck
Oh!
They need to be about 2 thirds down
Like this one?
Yes
What size?
I am a size 14, but my pink cardigan is a size 16 and it's
easier to put on, so get a size 16, what size is this one?
36
Oh, that's no good
I'll get a size 16
Don't worry, I'm asking for too much, I don't want to be
a nuisance
You're not being a nuisance
It needs to be 100 per cent wool
I'm not sure whether BHS would do 100 per cent wool,
would it?
Don't worry you're not experienced in shopping for an
old woman, I've got a catalogue that has just what I
want

Liz Bentley

Waiting for Aunt Margaret to die

Aunt Margaret has ovarian cancer, it's called the silent killer

She smells like she's already dead

My sister's a vet's nurse and farmer's wife but when she came to see Aunt Margaret she retched

She looks like a Gruffallo who has survived Auschwitz
 A Gruffallo is a monster in a children's book. Auschwitz is Auschwitz

I had to wear apron and gloves
 I was glad I didn't have to touch her
 One time she wanted the bedpan and wanted me to stay with her while she did it

She doesn't want to die
She doesn't want morphine
I asked her "do you want to die?"
"No" she said

My sister and I are registered next of kin
 No one else visits

One friend has come to light though,
A French woman, Auschwitz survivor living in East Grinstead, she has been scouring the Telegraph Obituaries for years

My mother (Margaret's sister) won't visit Margaret because when she had her stroke and was in hospital for 8 weeks she didn't visit her

If Margaret lives for more than 8 weeks in the hospital,
there are odds on that she still won't go

For three years I visited Margaret monthly, family duty
After I'd sorted her banking and post she'd say, "you
can go now"

My final visit is the worst
I don't know what to say to her
She knows I'm there but I don't know what she wants to
hear
I tell her about the children, my son, his sister, her
sister, my sister
She moves her fingers and I'm wondering if she's had
enough, if she wants me to go, if she wants to sleep
now

I say, "You can go now"

The nurse asks whether I want a call in the night
I say no
My sister says no
Her sister says no

Liz Bentley

My aunt gave my sister £14,000 and I got nothing

"I'll send the cheque back" she said, bluffingly

I told this story at a gig and a man in the front row gave me 5 euros

"I'll make sure my sister gets half" I said

I took off my top and he gave me another 5 euros

Buses from Auschwitz – Krakow

15.05
15.40
16.20   daily
17.00
17.30

Church Parade

I'm walking down the high street
In this uniform
With this flag

I think I've been spotted

Birth Story

Thank God it's nearly over; it's been really stressful here these last few months, growing, sudden UV lighting and shit music.
If I ever hear "Building baby's brains" and Mozart one more time I'll do a stillbirth.

I wish she hadn't given up smoking. I could do with a fag and I could murder a drink. Three glasses of shit CAVA at a wedding then dealing with her guilt for 8 months. That was worse than the gastro enteritis.

I'm really looking forward to going through that deep dark tunnel and getting into the pool. Soon I'll be pissing in someone else's water rather than my own stinky sac, and it's getting pretty stinky in here. Just got to hold off from shitting, just for a few more minutes otherwise it could all go horribly wrong and I'll end up with Dr Bari doing a caesarean, that's what happened to my brother and he's never recovered. They took him to a cranial osteopath but he's still got a flat head.

I've done my stretch in this old cell. Some have made it through the other side, some haven't. It's pretty hardcore to survive in these conditions. It's dark all the time and very basic. She could have done it up a bit; she's 41, she's had plenty of time, some pictures on the womb wall, wouldn't have to be anyone too raunchy, Helen Mirren perhaps. An internal tattoo would have been nice but maybe that would have stopped my concentration and deep exploration of my inner child.

Thank God the sex stopped. Most unsettling. Then all of a sudden it began again and she started taking it up the arse. That was only two weeks ago and by then it

Liz Bentley

had got so tight that I couldn't move around, my arse
was right by her arse. Just my luck I'll develop a liking
for it.

I think I'll be a poet when I grow up.

I'm a baby stuck in a womb
I'll be out soon
Thank God they rolled the dice again
Otherwise Boris would have been my name
Apparently Boris Johnson's buttocks are similar to those
of Adolph Hitler's
I heard that at a gig she did
That's when the arse thing kicked off and my kicking
stopped
Now it's my turn to help her out
Otherwise she'll have to shout – more
So, here we go, I'm really shitting myself now

Breastfeeding

My breast pump arrived from John Lewis
It's yellow and matches my living room walls
And the loo is the same colour

My friend told me that the yellow that shines so brightly
from my living room walls
Matches that of the yellow that shines so brightly from
Mc Donald's
You can't steal toilet rolls from Mc Donald's anymore
because they're all locked up
But you can steal free bibs and in the summer
If you are doing a barbeque
And you want free ice
If you tell them it's for charity
They'll give you some

Breastfeed, breastfeed, breastfeed, breastfeed all
through the night

I'm addicted to Deal or no Deal. I asked a friend
whether that was sad
He told me he thought it was a very clever programme
But that didn't answer my question
Do you remember Blind Date, when they did the older
people?
And you thought 'oh no, it's the older people'
I watch Blind Date repeats on Sky and when it gets to
the older people
I love it
 And laugh out loud

Breastfeed, breastfeed, breastfeed, breast feed all
through the night

Liz Bentley

Now I have insomnia, so I get up and write award-winning poetry like this

Breastfeed, breastfeed, breastfeed, breastfeed all through the night

£500 A Line and Other Poems

Outside Bermondsey Health Centre

Two pit bull terriers looking like their owner
Shat simultaneously right outside the health centre

"Ur" I said "haven't you got a bag?"

"Naw," he said

"That's disgusting" I said
"I had the biggest greyhound in the world and I got into it
The biggest poos in the world but I still got into it"

If I were judgmental, I would have thought his father had
abused him as a child and that he was a member of the
BNP
But I'm not judgemental. I just think he was a cunt

(One of the no no's of writing is apologizing to your
readers for your work, I would like to apologize for
apologizing and apologize to any readers that may have
been offended by me using the word cunt. I wasn't
thinking of a vagina when I wrote the poem. I am a
typical Essex girl, I had lots of sex, then I started school,
then I had lots more sex and truly valued my vagina less
than a packet of chips. You may argue that I have
taken myself out of Essex, and should somehow work
with the literal of literary. However as my writing comes
from primitive emotional torture I have not as yet been
able to take Essex out of the girl. I have indeed tried.
This is an excuse for being who I am. What I am
actually apologizing for is being alive. I have tried to kill
myself in more subliminal ways; like joining the
dangerous sports society in the days where safety
issues weren't the thing and having unprotected sex
with more men than Tracey Emin could fit onto her tent

in the 1980's, but I seem to have resided myself in trying
to live, yet with an internal death wish)

Sewing Lessons

We were sewing aprons with Mrs Clutterbuck
Using Bernina sewing machines, we liked it very much

"Oh my laddered stockings, what colour are they today?
Michelle you have such golden locks
That would go with yesterday's socks - but not today
My stockings are dark brown today

Who has dark brown hair in the class?
Stop what you are doing girls I need to find a match
So I can detach a few hairs to darn my stockinged feet
Elizabeth! Stay on your seat. Your hair colour is good
The colour of this wood (of the desk) it will match. Lets
detach"

She bustles back to her teacher's seat
Darns her stockings with my dark brown hair – there
Leaving me with a bald patch, which took time to recover

I have the apron I made in that class. I made two pockets
on either side
The others couldn't be arsed and put one large one in
the middle

Mrs Clutterbuck throws a hardwood blackboard rubber at
Haidee Fill
Which has broken her Bernina

Liz Bentley

I'm Happy

I'm happy, I'm happy, I'm happy, I'm happy
I'm happy too said Daisy who is three
I'm a bed cleaner said Oliver who is nine
I've never seen you clean a bed before
It was in 1776
You weren't alive in 1776
I am Jesus he said
If you were Jesus you could change this bath water into wine
Jesus shoots peoples heads off he said
I'm happy, I'm happy, I'm happy, I'm happy
And Daisy's happy too I said. I'm three she said
I'm Spiderman said Jesus
You're not Spiderman I said
Don't say it so loud, people will think I'm dumb and I can't write your poems for you, its too hard for me
I'm happy, I'm happy, I'm happy
I'm not happy anymore

Shy

I loved the Texas Chainsaw Massacre
I watched it in the loft of Gerald's house in South
Benfleet
His father owned the 2 sex shops in Southend
His father hung himself

My whip came from a shop in Kensington market but
was taken away from me in Corfu by a Greek man who
objected to my use of the whip in his taverna

Back in England, David Milligan gave me a lift home
from Reed Stenhouse Insurance where we worked. I
asked him to stop at the sex shop in Southend to buy a
replacement whip

The whips in Southend weren't of as good quality as the
whips in Kensington market. They were also more
expensive, but I didn't complain and bought one

I wanted to ask the shop assistant about Gerald's dad
and whether Gerald was ok but I was too shy

It was a hot day and the windows of David's Rover were
wound down. Holding my new whip I stretched my arm
out and let the whip blow in the wind down the A13 and
onto the A127 home

Bouncy Castle

My first school fête
Wanting to participate
Get to know some mums
Not sit on my bum

I did nothing for the school play, Xmas fair, Tsunami
benefit Sponsored Sing Along ,Charity Bike Race, Bug-
Finding Venture with Help the Aged and bug man Joe
Denture who wasn't a dentist in real life but a man of the
Church

My first school fête
A bouncer on the gate
Not the gate of the fête (selling raffle tickets for a prize
on the millennium wheel)
The gate of the bouncy castle doing its rounds of
Peckham estates and school fetes

Not just a bouncer, a technician too, keeping the holes
covered
Keeping the elastic band tied around the generator
Any more than twelve on at a time then the band
unwinds and we're into deflate
 Disappointed kids at the fête – can't have that

But it's not for long as we've been trained by the castle
men to tie those bands fast
Get back to who was in the queue last
But there's no queue, just bundles of colourful bodies

Then there's a fight - Peckham boys young but not light
Pulling them off to find a two year old in fright
A girl loses a tooth, blood spurts out onto the roof
Gum stuck on the sides and coins having free rides

£500 A Line and Other Poems

I have to find the tooth – forsooth

The girl is crying and her mother looks vicious
There's more blood on the floor the girl is forlorn
I can't see, but a tooth fairy has got there before me
I give the girl a pound coin from the float with the tooth
fairy quote
"I like Peckham school fetes - lots of teeth knocked out
for me"

The big boys are back but soon chucked off
Escorted off the grounds by large dads
Three hours of work and no break for a rice crispy cake
Just a run to the loo, no time to sit for a poo
Child's toilets you can see over the door, no privacy to
enjoy

At the end of the day, no I mean, at the end of the
afternoon
A bouncy castle bouncer will look good on my CV

The woman on the bric- a-brac relaxes and smiles
holding a glass of wine in the air
She sits surrounded with goods that nobody wants at a
fair
(Apart from a crochet toilet roll holder that I have my eye
on)

Staying alive

Lay down flat, on the mattress
No sex tonight, we're out to get bite, bit
By the bed bugs

Little tiny white ones, hungry baby white ones
Ah, bless 'em

Snuggle down, under the eiderdown
Sort of rhymes but not true
Really a du....
...vet

Glistening shiny pink ones
Don't splatter those ones, might be carrying baby ones
Ah, bless 'em

And the bed bugs sing -
Uh uh uh uh staying in bed, staying in bed
Uh uh uh uh staying in bed

Deep sleep, nightmares creep
Wake up and leap out of bed,
Light on, oh what fun inspecting
Bed bugs

Big dark daddy red ones
Juicy, juicy fat ones
Ah, bless 'em

Put them in a cigarette tin
Keep them alive for a day or so
Wash out the stains on the sheet if you can
Or die them red, passion for the
Bed bugs

Itchy, but nice, er than lice

And the bed bugs sing -
We don't fear death
Just excites us more
We like to grieve for our cousins
So
Don't worry

We make good pets
We're easy to keep
We don't affect your sleep and you are
Never ever, ever, lonely

So don't worry about us
We like to die
And you have much more in your life to worry about

And the coloured bed bugs sing –
Do, do do, do do, do do do do do do, do do, do do, do
do do do do
Do, do do, do do, do do do do do do, do do, do do, do
do do do do

Fridge Reminder

After we got back from Corfu, Marni went back after a
week cause she was bored in London. When she got
back the next week she led me to believe she'd had sex
with Rupert. She didn't actually say "I've had sex with
him" but she said they'd slept together and Jayne told
me that she knew they'd spent the night in her tent, but
she said that Rupert had just wanted to get close to me
and because I'd gone back to England he'd just got
friendly with Marni to get close to me. I know blokes
and I think she shagged him. Jayne asked why cause
she really didn't think so but I said that Marni was
jealous cause I was engaged to Nigel and she didn't
have a boyfriend and she didn't think it was fair to have
Rupert and Nigel, but I never actually had sex with
Rupert cause I was trying to be faithful to Nigel and
Chris the drug dealer, but Marni didn't know that and if
there is one thing best friends don't do and that is shag
anyone who their best friend has shagged. Jayne then
said that maybe we'd run out of blokes so we'd have to
shag each others, but I didn't think that was very funny
cause there were loads of countries we hadn't been to
yet, and I had a job and Marni hadn't so she was going
to hippy communes trying to find herself. 20 years later
Rupert married an English woman and moved to
London and I saw him in the Camden Head pub at a
gig, so I asked him whether he'd shagged Marni and he
said he hadn't. Then I wondered whether Marni had
said anything anyway; perhaps I'd imagined it, dreamt it,
but then I remembered, no, it was at Gay Pride when
she told me, we were pissed and on speed and I was so
upset I climbed up a pole in one of the dance tents in
Brockwell Park and had to be pulled down by fat
security men. My thighs were red, raw, burnt from the

pole - that's how hurt I was. So, I haven't asked Marni yet but I will next time I see her.

Bear with me

How am I driving?
I think you're driving well, so I take down your
registration and I dial 0800 101400. Compliments
should be impulsive, what a disappointment, when I'm
put on call waiting
I listen to Green sleeves for 95 minutes

I ring again, this time I am put through to April who has
a bear with her
We are in the month of April, how coincidently, eerily,
psychically, collectively unconsciously, spookily,
synchronized swimming

"GOOD MORNING CAN'T DRIVERS, MAY I HELP
YOU?"

"I was just ringing to say your driver was driving well"

"BEAR WITH ME" April put me on hold again

I listen to Ging gang goolie goolie goolie goolie watcha
April came back 15 minutes later

She asked me for my name, postcode, my house
number, a contact no, mob no, email address, details of
any websites I had. She asked me what the vehicle
was, it's colour, what the company name of the vehicle
was, what time it happened, "just now" I said, no she
needed to know the exact time "8.55 and 15 seconds
a.m." I told her

She asked, "SO HOW WAS HE DRIVING?" "I told
you, well"

"HOW WELL?" "Well, very well" "WAS HE
COURTEROUS" "Yes, he was courteous." "HOW WAS
HE COURTEOUS" "Well I was stressed and following
him had a calming effect on me
He came off the Old Kent road into Dunton road, he
pulled away from the lights beautifully
I followed him down the Dunton Road and he swung
graciously into Grange road, but not properly followed
him, I was going the same way as him, I didn't see his
face, it's not like I fancied him or anything, like I wasn't
stalking him"

"BEAR WITH ME"
I listen to Riders on the Storm for 13 minutes and 22
seconds

 April accused me of stalking her driver

I told her, "You have to believe me when I say I am not
doing this for my own gratification. I am in a relationship
already, it's turbulent at the moment, that's true, but I
am in one"

It is important to be told we are doing well in our jobs.
I should have rung April back to tell her how

The Affliction of Kings

My boyfriend's got gout
What's it all about?
Is it cause he's stout?
I doubt
It

He's just a red wine lout
He can't eat cheese, sardines or sauerkraut
Or trout

He gives me nowt
That's why I pout
I'm just gonna point him out
That's him
On his way out

He's got the gout
I've got the pout
Lets all shout
He's just shout
He's just banged his toe

Last night he went out
With the gout
Came home
Gave me a clout

He's given up the snout
Because of the gout
Taken up snuff
What's that all about?

I predict a diet

Herpes

Who got it first?
Not I, said the scout, with my sexual doubt
I not got it first

Twas I, said the Deptford punk
I laid the sore, with my didgery door
I laid the sore

But who took it on?
I took it on
Said the son of David Steel bursting balloons at the Spin
of the Wheel premiere
Where Jeremy Beadle cried on the stair and Bill Wyman
and Mandy signed autographs
I took it on

But who sustained the chain?
I said the dame, of Alice in Wonderland claim, but a
man all the same
With silver foil wall paper and ropes and chains
I sustained the chain, and maintained the pain

Who cleared it up?
I said the GU doctor at Southend-on-Sea General
hospital
Oooh.. that looks nasty, does that hurt? The nastiest
I've seen, where have you been? So many sores,
come, come students, adore!
We'll clear it up and won't tell your mum
Come out in a rash and we'll all keep stum

But no, look not afar
It's Mark with guitar
A local band, not doing bad, but legs crossed at the bar

Liz Bentley

It goes on we see
The Herpes

Hospital

Men in pyjamas wandering around corridors
Getting in lifts with them
Some with drips on wheels
I worry that the pyjamas or hospital robes are covering
their bits
I can't help but check, just in case
Then there's Trisha to watch on TV
I used to look forward to long waits in waiting rooms
Sitting quietly, reading a book, writing my life-story,
feeling my pain
Anticipating sharing my pain with you, sharing it with
you, fantasizing about sharing it with Trisha on national
TV.

Then it's back in the lifts, up and down
To see men in pyjamas or hospitals robes
Worrying about the drips on the floor

Liz Bentley

It's Shit

I went to Reading Rock in 1981
I met a Merchant seaman there from Durham
After the festival we agreed to meet
In Southend-on-Sea for a special treat
He didn't turn up so I went to the police
To report him missing – they laughed at me

I hate camping its shit
I hate camping its shit
I hate camping its shit
Especially with the kids

I went to Glastonbury in 1982
Hawkwind were at Stonehenge then I went there too
With a petrol-pump attendant at that time there were few
Now they're extinct but I met one in Corfu
Two years ago

I hate camping its shit
I hate camping its shit
I hate camping its shit
Especially with the kids

This year I was at Edinburgh staying in a flat
Performing in a tent, well fancy that
Now I'm writing this, for my new book
It may well read shit on paper

I've Only Got Myself to Blame

She sat on my coffee table
She thought it was a stool
I didn't like to tell her it was a coffee table
I didn't want to make her feel uncomfortable

And now it's broken
And I've only got myself to blame

Liz Bentley

Dear Madam,

Re :   Sexual health services/advice for young people
       Post of counselling supervisor

Thank you for your letter dated 28th September
informing me of my unsuccessful interview.

Obviously, on paper, I am extremely qualified for this
position. Otherwise there would have been no
interview. But unfortunately I had a gig the night before
and it was free beer and a very late night. I may well
have appeared stoned but I would like to put you in the
picture that that's just the breastfeeding and lack of
sleep. No drugs were taken (on this occasion).

I was indeed nervous when I arrived at your centre, I am
usually good at switching roles from comedienne to
therapist, but you guys just caught me out. I apologize
for calling your professionals 'you guys,' and when you
asked how I felt about abortion, what could I say? I
know so much about the subject I thought you would
have been able to read my mind and/or my CV and I
could only throw my hands up and say, 'Abortion.
Whey….'

I look forward to receiving your feedback.

Yours sincerely,

Liz Bentley

£500 A Line and Other Poems

Do you think eating the banana encouraged the man on the bike?

I haven't had any free time in months
The kids have been bundled and dumped
Off with child care
And I haven't a care

So off I go to the lido

It's hot in the car
But Brixton's not far
Far in my mind
All troubles left behind

So off I go to the lido

I get there on time
The parking is fine (that's unusual)
There is a sign
Lido open on 19th June
I don't know what the date is
Am I too soon?

Yes, it's closed

So what shall I do?
I haven't a clue
I text my friend
Go to Tooting he says
There's a lido there
But I can't get there
Take too long and childcare will be gone

So, I settle down and sunbathe, outside the closed lido
Watching other disappointed lido goers

This is nice, but there's no pool to pee in
I'll have to pee behind a tree
That's ok, no its not, there are no trees nearby that
would shelter me
And I don't want to miss more disappointed people
So I'll do it on the grass, and cover my arse, have got
plenty of water so the grass won't die

People stare and think, "Ha! She was here for the lido
and it's closed
Look she's laying on a towel in her bikini and she hasn't
got food cause she was gonna buy it at the lido bar,
over thar!"

A man on a bike asks me whether I'm young free and
single
I'm old have kids and a partner I say, I'm off he says
and is
"Try the internet" I shout to him
"I'm a Leo," he shouts back
"Wank," I shout back, and realize that it's far too hot a
day to be on the internet, I should have advised him to
go hang outside pubs.
He was a fool, a) I could have been lying, and b) had he
stayed we could have got talking, got to know one
another then I would have recommended him to one of
my friends

Those people thinking I had no food were wrong. Do
you think eating the banana encouraged the man on the
bike?

PC Turkey Lurkey

Turkey lurking in the freezer
Friends with children over for tea
"I'll get the ice-cream," says a mum
"No!" I shout, "I'll get it, don't look in there"
Nobody must see
Except you and me
Bernard Matthews has a nice smile
But his voice is sinister like a paedophile
No its not, that's a terrible thing to say
He's probably a really nice man and gay
No, I can't say that
He's just a nice business man who's into poultry

Your hair looks good

Your hair looks good
It must be the rain

Emergencies only

If you have a c section, it's got nothing to do with
erections
Of any sort, buildings etc.
But your baby will have a flat head
There are more flat heads now than there have ever
been, but the children you see in celebrity magazines
have their heads airbrushed

The graph of a health visitor

You're too tall - go cut some of you off
You're too small - go stick the cut off bit that's from the tall one, on you
You're too thin - I don't care if your mother and father were cats in a matchstick painting of cats and dogs, go drink cow's milk
You're too fat - I don't care if you are a fat cow
Go separate from your mother at birth and keep the countryside up

Tenants Association Meeting

I couldn't believe I had, such a lovely time
I couldn't believe I had, such a lovely time
I couldn't believe I had, such a lovely time
I couldn't believe I had, such a lovely time

Free childcare, wine and food and a prize draw
Free childcare, wine and food and a prize draw

I couldn't believe I had, such a lovely time
I couldn't believe I had, such a lovely time
I couldn't believe I had, such a lovely time
I couldn't believe I had, such a lovely time

Free childcare, wine and food and a prize draw
Free childcare, wine and food and I won £20 on the
prize draw

Planting Bulbs

I've been buying lampshades
Quite expensive too
But when I got them home today
The tag on the lampshades read
"No more than 60 watt light bulbs in us please"

I took an interest in lampshades because I recently won
one hundred 100watt light bulbs in my Housing
Association's quarterly magazine competition
I will now plant the light bulbs and the squirrels can have
them
I will break them up before I plant them and the squirrels
will choke on them
Serves them right for messing with my daffodil bulbs

My friend thought I didn't need to be so drastic and
showed me a book about squirrels and bulbs

Mac

I bought a mac, I bought a mac
And my friend told me I looked like a dinner lady in it

I bought a mac, I bought a mac
And my friend told me I looked like a dinner lady in it
But do I give a fack?

Oh yes

I bought a mac, I bought a mac
And I took that mac right back

I bought a mac, I bought a mac
And I took that mac right back

I've got a credit note that I must spend in May
I mustn't forget or it'll be like throwing money away
What shall I spend it on a birthday card or two?
A DVD of Pingu or a plastic doggy poo
They sell it all at this shop but the mac was on a rack
All on its own that's why I had to take it back
Not because the friend I mentioned told me it looked
crap

The mac was green and black
Bogie green and dark black
Now it's back on the rack
And I don't give a fack
About any more macs

Possible but Dangerous

H20 Fellatio
For the man reaching fellatio orgasm underwater, there is the danger of exhaling all the air in the lungs while still underwater and feeling the need to breath in sharply, which could cause panic or drowning if self-control is lost, but most men seem to be able to cope.

Massage and new relationships

My friend used to do a lot of massages but he stopped because he didn't think it was fair

Massage and old relationships

Massage and Masseurs

He seemed to be rubbing himself on the couch

Massage and Osteopaths that do a bit of massage

My friend's one told her that he had never seen such a nice bra before

Massage in the Maldives

The man had a woman and the woman had a man
At the same time doing the same things
Their fantasies were different

A massage for the exhibitionist where time doesn't mean money

A full back massage, not light aromatherapy in a dark room with potpourri and candles
A hard one in bright daylight with the smell of bean burgers at £12 an hour

A one-hour drive (sometimes more coming back), a trip to the massage chair at Reading services on the M4 is far better value for money

£13 in petrol (even in traffic) and £12 for the massage that's £23
A human massage (in private, in Peckham) costs £45 an hour
That's a saving of £22 to keep your body supple and free of back and neck pain

You need plenty of pounds coins. Insert them into the slot, and then relax
People look at you relaxing

He hasn't got planning permission

He hasn't got planning permission
For his extension
It would take one phone call to the council
And he would have to take it down

We got planning permission
For our extension
Building control came round and talked to our builder
about Top Gear for hours

Love Song

I'm in love with my son's primary school teacher
I think he loves me too

Every weekday morning my world has come alive with
love and romance.
I love him so much and I think he loves me too

His name is Chin
And he wears an earring
I think he's from Sri Lanka

I introduced myself to Chin.
I told him that I was Oliver's mother and that Oliver was
a little concerned that he didn't seem to know his name
yet

Chin told me that it was the second day of term and he
had 30 children's names to remember

That night, I asked Oliver whether Chin had
remembered his name that day
He had

It was parent's day last week. I was so excited. I put
my lipstick on and new knickers from Primark. I was
about to leave the house when my partner reminded me
that I would be in Reading tomorrow and Birmingham
Saturday, that would mean if I went out that night it
would be three days in a row I wouldn't be putting our
children to bed. He went

With global warming parents are sharing the drive to
school
I get to go to the school about 3 times every two weeks

I'm in love with my sons swimming instructor
I think she loves me too

My verruca fell off in the foot spa at Centre Parcs

I used to travel but now I can't be arsed
I go to Centre Parcs
An hour less than two no need to stop for the loo
I go to Centre Parcs

Deep in the remnants of the Daily Mails
There's one Guardian
I can't kill cyclists anymore
Because I am one

My verruca fell off in the foot spa at Centre Parcs

You can go naked in the aqua sauna
One couple did
They were German and had a lot of hair
Everywhere
I wish Jeremy Irons was there

I didn't mean it to happen
It just happened
I shouldn't have been in the foot spa
I should have been spending quality time with my
children
Playing outdoor adventure golf with plimsolls on
I should have taken medical advice and zapped it off
I've only got myself to blame

My verruca fell off in the foot spa at Centre Parcs

Slime Boy

I met Slime Boy in the swimming pool of the Peckham Pulse. We both swum furiously in the fast lane, but Slime Boy was being lane protective and not allowing me to over take him so I waited at the shallow end for his next completion of two lengths. I pretended I was adjusting my goggles, so he wouldn't suspect. As he approached the side, before he was able to tumble-turn, I dipped underwater and pulled at his trunks.

Slime Boy stood up. He tugged at my hand and separated it from his trunks and the manhood it protected. Oh, Slime Boy didn't look like he would ever need the 'I think I've got a small willy' therapy group, where men sit naked in a circle and look at the other members of the group, the out-come proving to be, confirmation and acceptance after at least two years group commitment and participation. Oh, Slime Boy would have been allowed to wear jogging pants instead of shorts at school.

And they call him Slime Boy. Slipping slipping, sliding sliding, squelching squelching slipping, I'm Jake the Peg diddle liddle liddle le, with my extra leg, diddle, diddle diddle de….

I said to him - "When I need to overtake you, you get in my way and swim across the lane, making my swimming experience one of stress and aggravation. Dr Payne told me this form of exercise would help my stress levels, therefore making my anxiety, panic attacks, dizzy spells and manic behaviour more tolerable."

"Oh dear," he said, "but, what a coincidence, Dr Payne told me that too!" He laughed.
"It's not a coincidence, Dr Payne see thousands of patients. I don't believe in coincidences, unless it's something to do with months of the year."

Whatever, it was true. Slime Boy had been told the same by Dr Payne - but for him, it was impossible to separate his outside experience. His psychology followed him into the swimming pool. But Slime Boy didn't want me to think this an excuse for his behaviour. He wanted me to understand and bear with him, he wanted unconditional positive regard, he wanted congruence and he probably wanted me to tell him how big his willy was.

I left him looking dejected in the shallow end and swum two lengths of butterfly, filling the lane.

On return to the shallow end, he said, "I knew I shouldn't have come here. I should just go back to swimming in my mother's pool."

How very exciting, I thought. This man must not be from round here. His mother has a swimming pool. I could marry into money and large penises.

"How old is your mother?" I asked
"89," he said. She'll be dead soon, I thought.

"Listen," I said. "I'll go with you to your mother's pool, we can swim together there, and that will make up for the stressful time and the fifty pence entrance fee I have wasted today."

"Alright," he said.
"What's your name?" I asked.

""I'm Slime Boy," and he shook my hand.
"You can call me John Winston that's my womb name."
Slime Boy started to cry. "Please don't talk about
womb's," he said.

And they call him Slime Boy, slipping slipping sliding
sliding squelching squelching embryo , bryo bryo bryo I
don't mean the brio that children play trains with I mean
bryo bryo bryo

I was disappointed to find that Slime Boy's mother lived
in Peckham on an estate that looked very much like my
own. From the outside it looked like a purpose built
suburban granny bungalow, built for the old lonely and
isolated. From the inside it looked like a purpose built
suburban granny bungalow, built for the old lonely and
isolated. But there was no central heating and it was a
cold day.

Slime Boy told me his mother had developed a bad
case of arthritis. Twelve years ago, after exhausting the
rheumatology department of Kings College Hospital and
downing all known forms of anti-inflammatory and
steroid treatment, Dr Payne could now only recommend
swimming. Slime Boy was distraught, he was forever in
debt to his mother for not aborting him. Although
abortion was illegal at the time, Slime Boys father was a
builder and knew a surgeon. But no, Mrs Bingley took
the money and kept it. Slime Boy, like his father,
became a builder. He was granted permission from the
council to build the swimming pool on the side of the
bungalow. Apart from windows, he stole most of the
materials from work. It took him 3 years to build.

We stood at the door and eventually his withered
mother let us in.

"I've been expecting you. It's in here," she said pointing with a joint swollen finger to a small door.

We walked into the room. It was dark - there were no windows. Slime Boy turned on a lamp that was perched on a small table by the door but it gave little light and there was little space to move around the pool so we took off our clothes where we stood. We didn't put on our damp costumes, we went into the pool naked, but it was too dark to see Slime Boy's third leg in its glory.

Slime Boy lowered himself into the stench that looked like professor gangrene-type excretions. He held his arm out to me.

"Come," he said, and I walked into the slime.

And they call him Slime Boy
Finger nails scraping off the grime, Slime Boy

The pool wasn't big, and with the grime it was difficult to swim properly, but I managed a few lengths of front crawl.
I changed my stroke to breast and on the third breast I felt like I'd kicked something. I kicked again, without the breast movement. It felt like the skin of a limb. I screamed.

And they call him Slime Boy,
Scrape, scrape away, someone will come another day

Slime Boy splashed out of the water in front of me holding a large plastic leg that he told me belonged to his mother's doll that she used for life-saving exercises, but I wasn't convinced. We swam small lengths. When I thought I'd got my 50p's worth I hauled myself out of

the pool and semi dried myself with my semi dry towel
and put my clothes back on.

"Thank you Slime Boy. I'm going now," I said.
"Oh, do you have to?" he asked in a sad squeaky voice

I nodded and pulled at the door but it wouldn't open. I
looked for Slime Boy. He was immersed back under the
slime. My eyes were becoming used to the darkness
and I noticed that the slime was now overflowing out of
the pool. I pulled harder at the door, shouting for Mrs
Slime Boy. I was panicking.

"John," called Slime Boy, "Don't worry, she's probably
killing us, I think that she thinks that you will take me
away from her." He laughed and the slime rose.

Slime Boy was wrong. The slime began to subside and
slip back into the pool. A temporary blockage, probably.
Minutes later, Mrs Slime Boy came to greet us again,
this time carrying tea and chocolate rice crispy cakes
she had made out of cornflakes.

Liz Bentley

There's no such thing as a free Bug Katcha

Last night, in the corner of the bedroom, nearest the door, furthest from my bed, something was moving. It was moving down the wall.

It was eye level with me.

In my flat, no matter what else is going on in my life, there's always a part of me that feels safe. A big, fat, hairy spider had just shifted that sense of security and I knew I wouldn't be able to sleep even if I didn't have insomnia that particular night. It was ten o'clock pm. The spider had to go.

I used to have a partner who got rid of spiders and bugs, but he's dead now, so I thought I'd get the nice man from the flat downstairs. I don't know him well, but a few weeks ago my shower tiles fell off and water leaked through to his ceiling. The man was nice, even though it was clearly my problem. Since then, he has smiled at me when we bump into each other on the stairs.

I checked that the spider was stationary before I left my flat and walked down to the next floor.

I knew the nice man lives at number twenty-seven because I'd seen him go in. I knocked on the door. There was no reply. Our flats are located under a flight path so he might have been wearing earplugs. I knocked again.

After a fifth, and final desperate bang the nice man's head appeared around the door. He looked tired. I thought, "I've got you up."

"Oh," he said. I noticed his face was flushed and he looked guilty, as if he'd been caught masturbating. He was wearing a frayed towelling dressing gown, he was breathing heavily.

"Did I wake you?"

"No, no," he panted. "I was doing my ironing." His clothes never look ironed.

"I'm going to a funeral tomorrow," he said.

"Whatever. Listen, I need you to come up to my flat, now, quickly. There is a large spider I have to get rid of."

"Are you scared of spiders?"

"No," I say. "Course I'm fucking scared of stupid spiders." You stupid, stupid man.

"Oh," he smiled, "I wouldn't have thought you were scared of anything."

"Please. Will you help me?" I was beginning to panic. The spider might have moved. It could have gone anywhere.

"Of course," he said. "I'll put some clothes on."

I almost told him not to bother – it would be wasting time. Then I thought better of it. The man is nice, but nice only. He disappeared inside his flat, leaving the door ajar and I waited outside.

I'm not scared of anything - apart from spiders. When I was a child, I used to be scared of daddy-long-legs as well. Little boys at school used to throw them at me.
One summer, my father sent me on a brownie pack holiday. It rained all week long so we spent our time in tents reciting brownie promises and singing Gang Show Songs. We slept eight to a tent and late one night, we had a visitor.

The daddy-long-legs was first seen flying around the tent by one brownie who screamed. Then we all screamed. Then, I stopped screaming, listened to the others, and thought how ridiculous it was.

I became 'Super Brownie', and caught the insect in my bare hands. I crawled out of the tent, and released it into the night air into the direction of a bonfire where a baked bean can was waiting to explode.

Oh how brave I was. I was congratulated by Brown Owl, Tawny Owl, Barn Owl and Little-eared

Screech Owl. The baked bean can exploded into the body of the daddy-long-legs whilst embers from the fire shot into our tent and some brownies were scarred for life.

My bravery was soon forgotten. I went back to school after the holidays and planted daddy-long-legs' into little boys' lockers. Mrs Longbottom caught me and gave me the plimsole. It didn't bother me, because I was no longer afraid of daddy-long-legs'.

The nice man was taking ages.

"What are you doing?" I shouted through the door.

"Coming," he said. Yuck.

The nice man appeared looking like superwoman, with pants over his trousers.

We rushed up the stairs into my flat and ventured into the bedroom cautiously, like Ghostbusters. I pointed to where the spider was.

"It's gone," I say.

"Look," the nice man whispered and pointed towards the floor.

The spider had crawled down the wall, onto the floor and camouflaged itself onto my shirt, about three feet away from our feet. Mr Spider was nestling into the shirt's collar.

"Ah," the nice man cooed and admired the spider, lovingly. "It's big isn't it!"

"Yes, It's big, fat and hairy and you have to get rid of it. Now."

"I'm not going to kill it."

"Doesn't matter. Just get rid of it."

He continued admiring Mr Spider. He wasn't reacting quickly enough. I was frightened the spider would run away or envelop itself so deeply in the shirt it might get lost in the removal.

"Quickly," I said.

"I don't think I want to pick it up. It's really big."

The spider wiggled its protruding leg, placed it on the floor and its remaining legs followed and climbed off the shirt.

The spider was moving towards me. Then it changed direction and began moving along the floor back towards the door and escaping into the hallway.

I screamed. The nice man was out of the bedroom chasing it. I slammed the bedroom door shut.

The nice man started making weird noises then it went quiet.

"Have you got it?" Silence.

"Have you got it?"

I heard the front door open and close. A few minutes later the door opened and closed again.

"It's alright," he said. "It's gone."

"What have you done with it?"

"It's outside. I put it out the window."

"Which window?"

"The hallway window"

"What hallway window?" My hallway doesn't have a window.

"I mean the landing window."

"What landing window?" My landing doesn't have a window.

"Down the stairs. Can I come in now?"

I leant on the bedroom door. I didn't wholly trust the nice man. I turned, faced the door and gently opened it.

I said. "If you tease me, I'll kill you."

He stood with his hands open in front of him. They were sweaty, but empty.

"I told you," he said. "It's gone."

The nice man looked sincere, but my threat to kill him had made him uneasy. His hands were shaking but he moved them towards my eyes for me to inspect.

"It's alright, I believe you."

My father used to chuck his fag ends out of the car window. They would often fly back into the car, land on the back seat and burn large holes in the foam seat coverings. When I started smoking and driving, I made sure the car window was fully open and I wouldn't throw out my butts until my arm was fully extended and the butt was pointing in the same direction as the wind. Speed and gravity, it works.

I screamed and slammed the door shut in the man's face.

He had thrown out the spider, but like a bunjee jumper, it had bounced back onto his arm, grabbed on for dear life, then climbed up the inside of his sleeve, along his shoulder then out on full display via his collar. I was watching Mr Big, Fat, Hairy spider looking bigger, fatter and hairier than ever, crawling up the nice man's naked neck.

"I'm not teasing," he said. "It's gone."

"It's not gone! It's on your neck. It's on your neck!! It's climbing up your neck you stupid, fucking stupid little man." I scream.

He screams.

"I've got it, I've got it."

"Hang on to it, just don't let it go. Don't forget I'll kill you. There's a bucket in the kitchen. Put it in the bucket, cover it with a tea towel, take it down the lift, out of the main door and don't come back until you've taken it at least a hundred feet away from the flats."

He came back later, mission accomplished. I hoped he would go straight home.

"I put it on a tree," he said, hovering at the door, holding the bucket and tea towel.

"Thanks," I say, willing him to go home. But he didn't.

"I'm not a stupid little man," he said.

"I didn't mean it," I said.

"Take it back then."

"You're not a stupid little man."

"Thank you," he said, still hovering at the door.

"Would you help me now, please?"

"How do you mean?"

"I want someone to talk to. It's my mother's funeral in the morning."

He lunged at me. Before I had time to push him off his arms slid down my body and he collapsed in a heap on the floor, holding onto my feet and sobbing. Poor Mr Nice Man. I pulled my feet away from him and sat on the sofa. He joined me and wept for hours. He left in the morning as the postman arrived.

The bereaved man had emotionally exhausted me. I sat back on the sofa with my junk mail.

Among the letters there was a small catalogue. I flicked through its pages, a light relief from dead mothers. I noticed an advertisement –

"Bug Katcha – Keeps spiders, flies etc at arms length with this unique product. Simply place the head of the Bug Katcha over the insect on a wall or window then twist the unit around so that the open shutter falls to trap the insect. Once trapped, the insect or spider can be released outside the home – safely and hygienically."

I placed an order. The Bug Katcha costs five pounds and ninety-nine pence. I wouldn't normally spend money on such a gadget, but it was an investment.

Liz Bentley

Swimming with Jeremy Irons

I was at the Peckham Pulse swimming baths when I
noticed a man who looked just like Jim Morrison
When I swam a little closer, he didn't look quite so much
like Jim Morrison as I'd thought, but never the less
I thought I would tell him that I'd just swallowed some
water, thinking that he would then link this to then
thinking that I would swallow his come
I would then acknowledge his thoughts and tell him that
I don't do swallowing come unless it's completely
necessary like, for example, I'd been on a desert island
for days and was really thirsty
After that I'd report him to the lifeguard who would expel
him from the centre and he'd have to go to Wavelengths
in Deptford
When you get up close to the lifeguard he looks just like
Jeremy Irons' twin brother

Tattoo

If you sit still you will get a nice one

Snakes
Lizards
Birds

If you don't sit still you'll get shit

Betty boo
Mum, dad,
True love

I watch the tank. Fish are swimming. They have strings
of poo hanging from their bottoms
A woman walks in from the street holding a raspberry
ice pop over her mouth. She is having her lip re-
pierced. She knows from experience there is no
anaesthetic provided here

Fish bones
Scull and crossbones
Hate mail

Would all our customers please be patient, out artists
are like our toilets - one shit at a time

I sit down and wait for 15 minutes, then my name is
called

Behind the mirrored door there are jars of lambs hearts,
eyes and alien foetus's positioned neatly on shelves

'A tree,' I say.
'Not much call for trees,' he says

'I've drawn a picture, here!'

He sketches and I scan the room. Balanced on a jar of lamb innards is a photograph

'Who's that?' I ask
'That's my niece, she's one year old tomorrow,' he says
She looks out of place here but then he tells me she's got twelve fingers and the spare two are being removed tomorrow, on her birthday, a coincidence
'We'll put them in a jar,' he says. 'It's a family business'

His copy of my tree is perfect and he sticks the transfer on to my belly. I lean backwards, supported by a swivel chair and stare at the ceiling, blowing at the feathers of a dream catcher hanging from the ceiling

15 minutes later and the tree is complete. Green, with roots, fertile, solid and when I'm gone, it will still be there, but not for long, as I have requested a cremation

Thank You Universe

Thank you Universe for those beautiful hand embroidered pictures that Auntie Brenda made last Christmas that I forgot to thank her for.

Thank you Universe for our times of celebration, Christmas, New Year, Easter, Divali, all those wonderful bank holidays when we get together with our families. Thank you for the happiness and great joy it brings to us all.

Thank you Universe for the amazing gift of life, Jesus's life, Jeremy Irons's life - all life. Thank you to my mother and father for bringing me into this life.

Thank you for the wonderful education I had, without which I wouldn't have been told recently how unique my ignorance is.

Thank you for the joy of love, sex and sexually transmitted diseases that gave my sister and I something in common.

Thank you for my boyfriend Mark Sidnell for not walking me home from the pub on 29th July 1981 so that Janet Bloomfield could beat me up in confidence so I will never forget the date when Charles and Diana got married which often comes up in pub quizzes.

Thank you Auntie Brenda for never taking me to France like you promised because I eventually went to Paris via the Channel tunnel instead of a crappy old boat trip to Calais.

Thank you Princess Diana for dying on 31st August 1997 and making my day trip to Paris so much more exciting and memorable and making me want to thank Auntie Brenda even more.

Thank you Janet Bloomfield for apologizing for beating me up because you got the wrong person and thank you to my mother for giving me her passive-aggressive genes so I would forgive Janet Bloomfield but suppress my anger that then made my legs numb and my eyes blurred.

Thank you Dr Bari for diagnosing these symptoms as multiple sclerosis, without which I would not be driving my brand new motorbility Vauxhall Zafira 1.8 with air conditioning and power steering, complete with the blue badge for parking, the freedom pass and exemption from the congestion charge.

Thank you Ronald Mac Donald for providing me with soft white toilet paper for all the years I was unemployed and thank you Ronald Mac Donald for putting locks on your toilet roll holders, giving me the incentive to look for a job.

Thank you to my old flute teacher Mr Long (a short man who abused me at school), without him I would never have gone into therapy, psychoanalysed my MS symptoms away and found a career in therapy and thank you to all the other Mr Longs out there who keep me in employment.

And lastly, thank you Universe for the Rasta Father Christmas's that can occasionally be seen inside a whole peanut if you look really closely.

The Lost fart

Wafting fart, waft away, through the trees, through the clouds, up to the sky
Up to Mars, where water has been found
A fire was found in Peckham, but alas, the fire brigade were on strike
I felt sad

Lifts can't be used during fireman's strikes. This strike went on for some weeks during which time my thoughts went out to the disabled people, so I took tea and biscuits and coffee and sugar and sold them to the disabled people who were waiting by the lift at the bottom of the stairs of Peckham library, nice building, won a millennium award

Each day of the fire brigade's strike I made more money
Each day the disabled people's library debts increased

I felt sadder

It's cold, there's a draft
The lost fart wafts through the doors, into the library, slips up to the fourth floor, reads a book, and is found again

I'm wafting in the air
I'm wafting up the library stairs
A light brown film surrounds me
Some say I look like a tree

I'm wafting in the air
I'm wafting in the sea of life
Was lost but now am found
High above the ground - in the library

Who is this?
Sitting by
Drinking tea
Forlorn
Who is he?
I cannot see
But he is reading porn

I'm wafting in the air
I'm wafting by a man's wheelchair
He smiles at me with grace
I poof right in his face
In the library

He lights a cigarette
He puffs out so much smoke it hurts
He lifts it high above
And stabs me in the heart
I'm a dying fart

£500 A Line and Other Poems

Typing CSE Grade 1

The quick brown fox jumoed iver ther lazy dog
The quickm brown fox jukpeds over the sleeping lazy
dog
The quick brown fox jumped over the sleeping lazy dpog
The quick brown fox jumped over the sleeping lazy dog

I am typing at a speed of 65 words per minute
But if you take off the mistakes it works out at 40 words
per minute comma
In 1980 you could get a job in the civil service with that
speed
But in the interview they asked me what other buildings
in the street
Were owned by the civil service
I said Telephone House
They said that was wrong it belonged to British Telecom
full stop
My cousin did very well in the civil service until the
censorship some years ago
It all went tits up and so did his relationship
But he said they didn't share the same sense of humour
anyway

return

Liz Bentley

Weekly Appointment

We all jump in the bath every Monday at 7.00pm
When the nice psychotherapy student comes to do his
baby observation

Inheritance or no inheritance - that is the question

Don't be fooled if old Mrs Buckmaster asks for your full
name

Windy Day

The fireman asked us
"Has this tree fallen over before?"
I said I thought it had
But my five-year-old son said no
The fireman didn't know whom to believe
But thanked us for our time

Peas

Xmas is coming, I won't be getting fat
I'll be far too busy, playing with my twat
(sorry this is not the Peas poem)

Xmas is coming, bulimics don't get fat
I make sure the sick doesn't soil the bathroom mat

Back at the Xmas table, I'm smelling like a rose
But I've left a bit of puke that's hanging from my nose

Food glorious food, hot sausage and mustard
While we're in the mood, regurgitate the custard

Peas

On my plate one solitary brussel sprout is left
Dad talks of starving Africans and gives it to the pet
Dog who swallows it in one and puts it's head upon my
knee
I wipe my nose with a serviette and the dog crouches
down and pees

Eat the world, don't they know its Xmas cake
Eat the world, salivate and masticate the peas

We wish you a merry Xmas, we wish you a merry Xmas
We wish you a merry Xmas, and a happy new year
Let's throw up some figgy pudding, lets throw up some
figgy pudding,
Let's throw up some figgy pudding, and bring up good
cheer

Peas on earth good will to men

Family Fortunes

We asked 100 people
"If Princess Diana were alive today, would she have had
plastic surgery?"
You said "yes"
Our survey said
"Yes"

The Suicidal Farmer

The farmer's in his den, the farmer's in his den, e i e o
the farmer's in his den
The farmer wants a wife, the farmer wants a wife, e i e o
the farmer wants a wife
The wife wants a child, the wife wants a child, e i e o the
wife wants a child
The child wants a nurse, the child wants a nurse, e i e o
the child wants a nurse
 The nurse wants the farmer, the nurse wants the
farmer, e i e o the nurse wants the farmer
The farmer wants the nurse, the farmer wants the nurse,
e i e o the farmer wants the nurse

The nurse wants a young people's confidential family
planning clinic
The nurse wants one of those clinics, e i e o the nurse
wants a clinic
The clinic wants a counsellor

This counsellor wants the farmer, but not the real
farmer, a fantasy one
She doesn't want stains in Staines
She wants red ruddy cheeks and big strong hands
She wants his overalls down, but not all the way down
Just half the way down with one hand on his phone
She wants his hobnail boots, but not the mud
She wants tractor marks on her neck, not on her track

The fantasy goes like the farmer's subsidiaries go
He's not a farmer any more, he's a guardian of the
countryside
Another way of saying your career has died

The farmer's had his lot, the farmer's had his lot, e i e o
and now we hear the shot

My Great Big Green Bin

I really enjoyed cleaning out my great big green bin
I used a broom to get out the grime
It's so big I'm so small I nearly fell in

Some of my neighbours pay a small company to do it for
them
I don't know how much it costs it might be £10 a month
but that's not the point
A truck arrives after the refuse collection
But cleaning my bin gives me so much satisfaction

Flash, flash, it's clean in a flash
Flash, flash, it's clean using flash
I get inside and stay in for a while
My house is full, so is the shed
In the bin it's quiet as a mouse
In the bin it's not like the house

I went to B&Q to buy a roof light
So I can start reading in my bin
I've never read much
I didn't go to school much
Or college
I'm really out of touch

I'm going to stay in the bin for as long as I can
I did, but fell asleep and into a dream
I dreamt of a magic carpet that took me back to B&Q
There was a man, looked like my father
I wanted to read the instructions of a power drill
And he shouted "no, no
NO, NOOOOOoooooo"

Liz Bentley

I awoke with a filled Sainsbury's nappy bag landing on
my head
It was the morning poo of my baby
I'd been in there all night
My partner thought I'd probably met Jeremy Irons in the
pub
And decided to stay out

RMC   Suite 8, third floor

Didn't we have a lovely time at the recurring miscarriage
clinic
You must admit it's improved a lot with the new
consultant Mr Jerkoff
And when he's about the ladies shout aloud with glee
Didn't we have a lovely time, all of the girls and me

Big long shiny probe right up your fanny
Searching, searching in every nook and cranny, oh

Didn't we have a lovely time at the recurring miscarriage
clinic
You must admit it's improved we see with new
magazines and daytime TV
And when we all see a heavily pregnant celebrity
We all shout out aloud in joyous arouse, all of the girls
and me

Pictures of foetus's lining the corridor walls
Old ones, new ones and some in fallopian tubes, oh

Didn't we have a lovely time at the recurring miscarriage
clinic
You must admit it's improved the loss with the new
receptionist Mrs Toss
And when she's about the ladies shout aloud with joy
A fabulous time, I wonder what sex, a girl or a boy

La la la la, la la, la la, la la la la, la la….etc
Didn't we have a wonderful time at the Recurring
Miscarriage Clinic….

Orange Badge

Orange badge, orange badge now your blue oooo
Oooo I love you. But

Beware, of the loading bay bans beware of the loading
bay bans

But thank you God for the clever begger who sits on the
kerb by the loading bay
They save you £80, you give them 4, but don't clip their
leg when you shut your door

Red route, three hours wait, single yellow, double yellow
7 bridge, Dartford tunnel (both ways), designated bays

Beware, of the loading bay bans beware of the loading
bay bans

It Hurts

My Motorbility Vauxhall Zafira is automatic but it still has a gear knob
There is a chrome bit at the top of the knob that you have to push down to put the car into drive etc

In the summer when the knob gets really hot the chrome bit burns my fingers

Also, when the chrome bit that you push down is released, if my fingers aren't in the right position it pinches the skin and it hurts

I'm hurting, hurting, hurting,
I'm hurting, hurting, hurting, I'm really hurting

I rang up the garage and they told me it was no design fault. It was me
I feel so isolated. My sensitive fingers exposed and vulnerable

My friend said "go to the doctors get some CBT, Cognitive Behavioural Therapy"
He speaks in rhymes, I don't
"It works," he said, "and it doesn't hurt," he said
I look down at my red raw fingers and so did he
"You drive a lot, I forgot," he said

I'm hurting, hurting, hurting, hurting
I'm hurting, hurting, everybody hurts

Liz Bentley

My Paul Experience

Paul Barton in primary school; he asked if he could see
my vagina so I said if I could see his willy I would show
him.
He showed me his willy then I ran down the corridor.
My guilt followed me into senior school where I
smuggled flick knives from Calais to Dover on a school
trip, just for him. He didn't see this as payment from
before and kindly gave me a knife

Paul Ashton from Basildon; I gave him genital herpes.
He didn't have to have it. I told him I had sores, nasty
sores, but he insisted

Paul Watkins from Canvey Island bought me a Vox
Continental organ

Paul Mazda who played bass and injected heroin into
veins in his ankles at band rehearsals –he's now a
therapist, worked on the Trisha show for 7 years

Paul Marchant, my therapy teacher, who wasn't that
good - but he's dead now

Paul White taught me how to play Neil Young Heart of
Gold on the guitar

Paul, oh god, I can't remember his name, Benitses,
Corfu, gave good aqueous cunnilingus

Paul Benitses 1986, Paul Pelekas from Liverpool 1987,
me and Sandra both had him, he's written a book and
we were special

Rayleigh Methodist Church Magazine November 1987

Let us pray this week for poor Mary Bentley whose daughter has been struck down with the life crippling disease Multiple Sclerosis
Prayers go out to Mary and her family and friends who will have to care for her
Our collection this week will go to the MS society

Liz Bentley

Getting the 176 bus from Elephant and Castle to Leicester Square

188, I mean 1 188 not 1 88
A 171, a 172, a 177, 2 177's
A 63, 263 I mean 2 63's not 263 363
2 363's, 3 363's
A 100, a 45 where the fuck does that go to?
Shadwell
A 68 2 68's a 468
2468 A road

One with lights on
One with lights off
We could have got there quicker if we'd walked

There is a woman at the bus stop carrying two ironing
boards
I asked her why she was carrying two ironing boards
"They're for the home," she said

In the 1980's, opposite the Charlie Chaplin pub at the
Elephant and Castle
While we were waiting for the no 1 or 188 (destination
Surrey Docks) Kevin Robertson and I would fuck. At the
bus stop there was a fence, then some grass, then
some flats. We'd climb over and do it up against the
fence, the grass had too much dog shit on and it was
usually raining
Kevin was a great fuck despite his heroin addiction but
times got hard
He did a post office job and ended up in
HMP Saughton, Durham, Brixton, Wandsworth then
semi open Send in Woking
(in that order)

£500 A Line and Other Poems

The 176 is here
All the way from Penge

Doctor's Song

I've got a very good relationship with my GP
They change all the time but I don't care who I see
I get a regular prescription of temazepam
I am very, very, very, very, very, very, very, very, very,
very, very, very, lucky

Many, many, many people don't know
That prescriptions can always be free
They don't check what boxes you tick
Or if it's really you that's sick

Dr you can't cure me cause there's nothing, nothing,
nothing, nothing, wrong
I'm not sick just bored a bit and needed new material for
a song

*"dr dr, I think I'm dying of liver cancer, my skin's gone
yellow"*
*"don't worry, its not years and years of alcohol abuse,
you've just got Carotenemia, you eat too many carrots,
ha ha ha"*
*"it can't be, surely, no its not,I must be dying, but hey,
no, no, its not that, its this tinted moisturizer I've been
using ha ha ha"*

You get lots and lots and lots of money
But its changing rapidly so don't be smug
The surgery is now open till half past seven
No early break you've got a meeting at eleven
The Primary Care Trust are crushing, crushing,
crushing, crushing you
But Government Guidelines suggest that CBT will work
for you too

CBT will work for you CBT will work for you CBT will
work for you CBT will work for you
CBTCBTCBTCBTCBTCBTCBTCBT
Yes no yes no yes no no yes no yes maybe
occasionally sometimes no no sometimes maybe no
maybe take away take away take it away self service

CCBT That's computer cognitive behavioural therapy,
that's doing it with a computer but be careful you don't
press the wrong button because you could end up on a
porno site, one more wrong button and you could end
up in court accused of being a paedophile

CCBT2 That's computer cognitive behavioural therapy
2, this time you do it with a psychologist (probably about
the age of seven) who will help you learn how to work
the computer. Then there's -

SHB self help books, self help books, self help books,
do it yourself books, do it yourself, play with yourself

Dr you can't cure me cause there's nothing, nothing,
nothing, nothing, wrong
I'm not sick just bored a bit and needed new material for
a song

**Pre assessment forms in no particular order
February 2007**

Letter confirming appointment
Reply slip
Patient Registration Form
Cognitive Behavioural Therapy – what is it? (2 sides of
explanation)
Clinical Outcomes in Routine Evaluation (34 questions)
BDI   (21 questions in very small print)
PDQ-4+   (99 questions plus some questions have up to
15 other questions to them)
Thank you for your time

Inappropriate

Cancer ward
Lymphoma
Kings College Hospital, Camberwell
At Christmas time

Men who were dying
Barely surviving
Not allowed to come out of their cells
Infection swells

Apart from at Christmas time
Out for Christmas entertainment
Not carol singing in this instance
But Liz Bentley performance

I started to play
Already one wheeled himself away
Suicidal Farmer – not appropriate
Breastfeeding song – not appropriate
Killing a cyclist – not appropriate
My aunt died and gave my sister....
Not appropriate

These men out of their cells
Thinking they were now in hell
And I was in hell with them

I stopped, under-time
We talked
They talked
With masks on
For 50 minutes
Over-time

Liz Bentley

I had a cold
And hadn't been told
That that was inappropriate

Come on Baby Light my Boiler

My new boyfriend bought a tool belt
This weekend is going to be cold
That may mean that my boiler will need tinkering about
with